W9-BDB-125

The Shyness Workbook

30 Days to Dealing Effectively with Shyness

Bernardo J. Carducci

with Ronald J. Allman and Lisa Kaiser

Research Press
2612 North Mattis Avenue
Champaign, Illinois 61822
(800) 519-2707
www.researchpress.com

Copies of this book may be ordered from Research Press at the
address given on the title page.

Composition by Jeff Helgesen
Cover design by Publication Services
Printed by United Graphics, Inc.

ISBN 0–87822–551-X

For Dr. Philip G. Zimbardo, who has been a source of personal and professional inspiration, a mentor, and, most important of all, a most cherished friend. You sparked my interest in the study of shyness and gave me the courage to deal effectively with my own shyness. You changed my life for the better—forever. Thanks. I owe you one, Z.

Contents

Preface

Words of Welcome and a Plan of Action

As a shy teenager in college, I began reading about shyness in an attempt to help myself overcome it. Since then, my initial interest in shyness for purely personal reasons has turned into a professional pursuit that has captivated me for the past 25 years. In my quest to understand the nature and underlying dynamics of shyness, one of the most fascinating aspects of shyness that I have found is its pervasiveness. Specifically, my research, along with the research of others, indicates that approximately 40 percent of the general population describes itself as shy, and about 95 percent says it knows firsthand what it means to be shy in any number of situations. So chances are pretty good that either you are shy or you know individuals who are or have been shy.

A critical consequence of shyness is the pain and difficulty it can cause you and other shy individuals in the many and diverse areas of your lives that are central to your sense of happiness—for example, establishing friendships and intimate relationships, pursuing educational and career opportunities, and fostering personal and family relationships over a lifetime. The enduring pain of shyness was expressed to me one day by a woman over 80 years old who approached me after I gave an hour-long brown-bag lecture to a community group. With her eyes welling up with tears and her voice trembling, she said, "I wish I would have heard what you said when I was 10—not 80! I missed out on so much!" Although such a comment is heart-breaking, unfortunately, it is representative of the comments I hear all too frequently in the thousands of conversations I have with shy individuals and in the letters, e-mails, faxes, and phone calls I receive from shy individuals from all over the world. No doubt you have experienced sentiments about your own shyness that are similar to those expressed by the elderly woman who approached me after the brown-bag lecture.

Although shy individuals are often perceived as passive and withdrawn, my research indicates that many shy individuals are proactive in their efforts to implement a variety of self-selected strategies to deal with their shyness. However, a characteristic feature of many of these strategies is that they are based on an incomplete understanding of the underlying dynamics of shyness and, as a result, tend to work against the best interests of these shy individuals. Implementing such self-selected strategies can produce less than satisfying results; in turn, that leads to feelings of frustration and futility. Again, I have no doubt that most of you have tried many solutions to deal with your shyness that have left you feeling less than satisfied and a little more than frustrated, which is probably why you decided to utilize *The Shyness Workbook.*

Based on all that I know about shyness, *The Shyness Workbook* is designed to help shy individuals like you—as well as those of you who know shy individuals—to deal effectively with your shyness and to become "successfully shy." A basic premise of this workbook is that shyness is not a disease or a personality defect or a character flaw that needs to be treated. Rather, shyness is viewed as a characteristic feature of one's personality that, like all other aspects of a healthy sense of self, needs to be understood, appreciated, and taken into consideration when responding to the challenges of everyday living. For you and other shy individuals, the challenge is not to change who you are—remember: there is nothing wrong with being shy—but to change how you respond to your shyness. *It is about changing how you think, feel, and react to your shyness and developing strategies that are based on this understanding that work with your shyness instead of against it.* Successfully shy individuals learn to control their shyness instead of letting their shyness control them.

To help you and other shy individuals become successfully shy, *The Shyness Workbook* contains a series of 30 separate daily units designed to provide the type of information that will make it possible for all shy individuals to respond more effectively to their shyness. Each daily unit contains four elements. The first is titled "What You Need to Know" and includes some core information about shyness that is designed to help you focus on a central issue or critical feature associated with understanding the nature and dynamics of your shyness. The next element—"Your Turn"—contains a variety of self-directed activities and self-scoring quizzes and inventories designed to promote self-examination by the shy individual. Next is a feature titled "Voices." The "voices" contained in this feature are quotes from actual shy individuals that are designed to illustrate in a more personal sense the theme reflected in the core information discussed in the "What You Need to Know" and "Your Turn" features. These voices are also designed to let you and other shy individuals know that you are not alone in the types of thoughts and feelings you have, your trials and tribulations, and the stress of community and connectedness with other shy individuals out in the world. Finally, these three features (or elements) help you transition into the "Reflections" feature. This journal activity is designed to help you and other shy individuals think about what has been presented regarding the core information at the beginning of the unit, your responses to the "Your Turn" feature, and your reactions to hearing the other shy voices. Each "Reflections" entry includes a critical quote taken from the "What You Need to Know" section that captures the essential point being made in the lesson. The critical quote is also designed to help stimulate the process of self-reflection and expressive writing based on this reflection.

Much of the information presented in *The Shyness Workbook* is based on some of my more extensive writing on the subject of shyness, including *Shyness: A Bold New Approach* (HarperPerrenial, 2000a), *The Shyness Breakthrough* (Rodale, 2003), and *The Pocket Guide to Making Successful Small Talk: How to Talk to Anyone Anytime Anywhere About Anything* (Pocket Guide Publishing, 1999). Although *The Shyness Workbook* is designed to be used as a separate tool for helping you and other shy individuals understand and respond more successfully to your shyness, you may find it helpful to supplement your knowledge of shyness gained through *The Shyness Workbook* by reading the previously mentioned books.

So, as you begin your journey to become "successfully shy," please do not be shy about contacting me. I welcome your comments and look forward to hearing from you regarding your progress as you advance through the daily units of *The Shyness Workbook*. I can be reached by e-mail at shydoc@carducci.com or by sending a letter to me at this address:

The Shyness Enrichment Institute
P.O. Box 8064
New Albany, IN 47151–8064

I look forward to hearing from you. I wish you much success. Do keep in touch.

Best regards,
Bernardo J. Carducci, Ph.D.

Acknowledgments

Some Expressions of Gratitude

There are plenty of people who helped make *The Shyness Workbook* work. First of all, I want to thank the thousands of shy individuals whose courage to come forward and share their stories of shyness has been a tremendous help in my ongoing research into the nature and underlying dynamics of shyness. Their requests for assistance with their shyness have been a significant source of inspiration for creating *The Shyness Workbook.*

Ron Allman, a colleague at Indiana University Southeast, was always there to let me drop by his office for "just a minute" to talk about the workbook. Of course, that "minute" eventually turned into quite a few hours over the course of this project and led to many interesting discussions on topics ranging from shyness to university politics to world affairs, just to name a few.

Lisa Kaiser, my research associate and longtime friend, contributed by helping to make the voices of shy individuals be heard loud and clear, as she has done so well for so many years.

I am grateful to Marty Rosen, Gabrielle Carr, Jacqueline Johnson, Melanie Hughes, Bonita Mason, Joyce Owens, and especially Nancy Totten for being the kind of reference librarians who were there to help find "stuff" whenever I asked.

I also must acknowledge the "Lunch Bunch"—Lesley Deal, Brigette Colligan, and Kathleen Norvell—for making me laugh more in one hour between bites of fast food than most people do in a month.

Rozana Carducci, my daughter and soon-to-be member of the professoriat, served to keep me motivated with her calls to discuss my work, her work, and the joys of our father-daughter relationship.

Finally, at Research Press I owe a debt of gratitude to David Hamburg for his careful and insightful editorial advice and to Dennis Wiziecki and especially Russell Pence for their enthusiastic support of my work.

To all of these individuals, I say thanks for making my work on this workbook more like play than actual work.

DAY 1 Defining Shyness: What Shyness Really Is

What You Need to Know

First and foremost, shyness is not a disease that needs to be cured, a character flaw that needs to be eliminated, or a personality trait that one should find embarrassing. Nor is shyness synonymous with introversion. An introvert is someone who prefers solitary activities but can be social when the need arises, such as when attending public functions.

The shy individual is someone who truly wants to be with others but, for a variety of reasons, finds socializing difficult. To help clarify this distinction, although both the shy individual and the introvert may be standing against the wall at a party, the introvert is there because he prefers to be, whereas the shy individual is there because she feels she has no choice.

As this example illustrates, what shyness really comes down to is a matter of control. For shy individuals, their shyness controls them: It holds them back in terms of their careers, educational goals, and love lives. To overcome your shyness, you have to learn how to control your shyness instead of letting it control you.

Your Turn

The Shyness Quiz
For each item, circle the number of the answer that best fits you.

How often do you experience the feelings of shyness?

1. Once a month or less
2. Nearly every other day
3. Constantly—several times a day!

Compared to your peers, how shy are you?

1. Much less shy
2. About as shy
3. Much more shy

"Shyness makes me feel symptoms such as a racing heart and sweaty palms." This description is

1. Not like me
2. Somewhat like me
3. A lot like me

"Shyness makes me think others are reacting negatively to what I do and say." This description is

1. Not like me
2. Somewhat like me
3. A lot like me

"Shyness keeps me from acting appropriately in social settings—for example, introducing myself or making conversation." This description is

1. Not like me
2. Somewhat like me
3. A lot like me

"Shyness looms whenever I interact with someone I'm attracted to." This description is

1. Not like me
2. Somewhat like me
3. A lot like me

"Shyness looms when I'm interacting with someone in a position of authority." This description is

1. Not like me
2. Somewhat like me
3. A lot like me

To determine your score, add the numbers that you circled. Once you come up with your total points for the quiz, look at the following three ranges of numbers to see where your score falls. Then read the accompanying comments to determine what your score tells you about your shyness.

7–12—Any shyness you feel is normal. Usually you are not a very shy person.

13–18—You experience a lot of shyness in your life. This workbook will help you when you encounter these situations.

19–21—You are a very shy person. With this workbook and some hard work, you can overcome your shyness.

Voices

"It's like living in an invisible cage. You're trapped but no one else can see it. They're not aware of it but it's just crushing to your personality. You have no freedom and you're not actually chained but you don't have any choices. You stop doing what you want to do because you fear that others won't think that you're good enough to do things or be with others. I feel like there's always a spotlight shining on me, that I'm always under scrutiny."

—a college student in the Northeast

"Almost all of the people I know don't think that I'm shy, and when I say that I am, they kind of laugh it off because I don't act like the typical shy person. I express my shyness in a different way. For example, instead of being withdrawn or untalkative, I would rather make jokes or act silly or sarcastic."

—a 30-something homemaker

'The shy individual is someone who truly wants to be with others but finds socializing difficult.'

Reflections

Being a shy person gives you insight that someone who is not shy might not have. What is your opinion of the following assertion?

"The shy individual is someone who truly wants to be with others but, for a variety of reasons, finds socializing difficult."

_____

_____

_____

_____

_____

_____

_____

_____

_____

_____

_____

_____

_____

_____

_____

_____

_____

_____

DAY 2 Born Shy? A Basic Question

What You Need to Know

One of the most popular misconceptions about shyness is that people are born shy. Being born shy is an impossibility. The reason is that shyness involves a sense of excessive self-consciousness, negative self-evaluation, and self-preoccupation. Each of these critical elements of shyness has its basis in the presence of a sense of self, which begins to develop in infants when they are about 18 months of age.

There are some infants born with what is called an "inhibited temperament," which means these infants display excessive emotional and physical responses to novel stimulation. One example of this is a six-month-old infant who displays excessive physical and emotional responses to novel stimulation, such as the ringing of a bell. Another example is a three-year-old child who clings to her parent whenever a stranger enters the room and tries to interact with the child.

The expression of such an inhibited temperament early in life does not guarantee that such individuals will grow up to be shy adults. Even if it did, all it would mean is that such individuals would have to make decisions about how and where to socialize that would take into consideration their temperament (e.g., go to a poetry reading instead of a loud bar). The notion that people are born shy is simply a *belief* about shyness, not a *fact* about shyness.

Your Turn

First, describe why shy individuals might believe that people are born shy. Next, describe some of the factors you feel have contributed to your shyness.

_____

_____

_____

_____

_____

_____

_____

_____

_____

_____

_____

_____

_____

_____

_____

_____

_____

_____

Voices

"I think life experiences can make a person shy, but I strongly believe that shyness is something I was born with. I believe that certain experiences added to the intensity of my shyness. I think that I was born a 'truly shy person' but my shyness either increased or was lessened by how I reacted to certain life experiences. I think having overprotective parents had a lot to do with my shyness as a child. Being shy as a child wasn't as bad as it was later in my life."

—a 28-year-old graphic designer

"Even at the age of three or four, I was very self-conscious about my shyness, and I'll always remember that I couldn't wait to get older because I thought that I would grow out of it. Little did I know that the older I got, the worse the problem got."

—a 55-year-old dentist

"One of the most popular misconceptions about shyness is that people are born shy."

Reflections

How do you feel about the following statement?

"One of the most popular misconceptions about shyness is that people are born shy."

_____

_____

_____

_____

_____

_____

_____

_____

_____

_____

_____

_____

_____

_____

_____

_____

DAY 3   Shyness Is Not All in Your Head: Putting It in Perspective

What You Need to Know

Shyness is not a mental defect, a neurosis, or an emotional disorder. Rather, it is a characteristic feature of personality that is holistic in nature—involving the body, the mind, and the self of each shy individual.

The experience of shyness includes physiological reactions in your body, such as a racing heart and a dry mouth; thoughts in your mind, such as the feeling that others are judging you negatively; and a view of your self that includes conflicting emotions about your identity and self-esteem.

If shyness occurred only in your head, it would be easy to alleviate. All you would have to do to put an end to your pain and suffering would be to think different thoughts. Because shyness is such a comprehensive experience, quick-fix remedies such as breathing exercises or positive thinking ("Go to your happy place") will never work because they are superficial and fail to consider the complexity and holistic nature of the experience of shyness.

To ensure that you appreciate the holistic nature of shyness, the strategies offered in this workbook incorporate your mind, body, and self. Looking at your shyness holistically helps you to develop a comprehensive and personalized plan to assist you with the unique way in which you experience your shyness.

Your Turn

List a few beliefs you have about shyness and the effect those beliefs have had on your life.

	Beliefs	**Effects**
1.	_____	_____
	_____	_____
	_____	_____
	_____	_____
2.	_____	_____
	_____	_____
	_____	_____
	_____	_____
3.	_____	_____
	_____	_____
	_____	_____
	_____	_____
4.	_____	_____
	_____	_____
	_____	_____
	_____	_____

Voices

"My shyness is expressed as quietness. I rarely initiate social contact even with my friends. I am usually terrible at making small talk and don't put out much effort to improve this. I have somewhat jokingly described myself as a hermit living in a city, but there's certainly a lot of truth to this."

—a 41-year-old claims adjuster

"Even when people try to be friendly and reassuring, I have a hard time making eye contact. During conversations my mind goes blank. I stand there mute, filled with misery. If any words are jarred loose, they come out fragmented or incoherent. Sometimes words spill out, but they are inappropriate because the conversation has moved on to something else. Most of the time I don't say anything, and then I come home ready to explode with all the things that were left unexpressed. My frustration is so great at times that it takes a lot of effort to calm down."

—a 55-year-old homemaker

"If shyness occurred only in your head, it would be easy to alleviate."

Reflections

How do you feel about the statement below?

"If shyness occurred only in your head, it would be easy to alleviate."

_____

_____

_____

_____

_____

_____

_____

_____

_____

_____

_____

_____

_____

_____

_____

_____

_____

_____

DAY 4 Understanding Approach-Avoidance Conflict: The Source of the Pain

What You Need to Know

The principal source of pain for shy individuals is the approach-avoidance conflict. Assuming you are the shy person, here is how this well-known conflict plays out: You have a simultaneous and equally powerful desire to want to approach others and also to avoid them. For example, you might want to meet new people at social events or make your views known to others at a business meeting; however, fearing that you and your ideas will be evaluated negatively, you decide to avoid one or both of these situations entirely.

When you become caught up in this approach-avoidance trap, your heart tells you to be with others, while at the same time your head orders you to avoid them. You desire social contact but doubt your ability to succeed at it. You want to be accepted and understood by others, but you hold back from expressing yourself fully. You are afraid of being judged, so you figure the safest course is not to say or do anything or possibly to avoid others altogether.

Unfortunately, the more you want to be with others and the more your shyness holds you back, the greater the personal pain. This is the essence of being caught in the grasp of the approach-avoidance conflict. In time, you will see that a critical element of the approach-avoidance conflict is your ability to tolerate risk.

Your Turn

Assessing Your Tolerance for Risk

On a scale of 1 (totally uncharacteristic of me) to 5 (totally characteristic of me), rate yourself on the following statements and circle the number after each statement that you feel best represents you:

1. It's easy for me to approach total strangers at a social gathering and begin conversation.

   Uncharacteristic   1   2   3   4   5   Characteristic

2. I enjoy being the center of attention.

   Uncharacteristic   1   2   3   4   5   Characteristic

3. If I disagree with someone, I will let him or her know.

   Uncharacteristic   1   2   3   4   5   Characteristic

4. I don't mind being one of the first people on the dance floor.

   Uncharacteristic   1   2   3   4   5   Characteristic

5. I usually don't worry about being rejected for what I do or say in public.

   Uncharacteristic   1   2   3   4   5   Characteristic

6. If I'm attracted to someone, I let him or her know.

   Uncharacteristic   1   2   3   4   5   Characteristic

7. I don't mind going to a social gathering alone.

   Uncharacteristic   1   2   3   4   5   Characteristic

8. I look forward to meeting new people at social gatherings.

   Uncharacteristic   1   2   3   4   5   Characteristic

9. I don't worry about committing a faux pas because most people will forget what I do wrong.

   Uncharacteristic   1   2   3   4   5   Characteristic

10. I usually don't hold my feelings back when I'm interacting with others.

    Uncharacteristic   1   2   3   4   5   Characteristic

The higher your score (25–50), the more likely you are to take risks with other people. If you scored on the low side (10–24), you're probably avoiding new encounters because you believe they're too unpredictable and dangerous. The key is to take calculated risks by planning for challenges.

Voices

"I have left social gatherings without telling people, no matter what the consequences, even if I had to walk all the way home in the middle of the night. I avoid social situations almost totally. I become tongue-tied around others, and very quiet. If the situation is intense, my hands will sweat and I feel nauseated."

—a 30-year-old school bus driver

"My old thinking was, What do the other people get out of this association, and why would they do this for me? This would prevent me from approaching others—personally, socially, and professionally. Now, I am able to approach people or ask them to do things for me. I'm more social and don't hesitate much to go into a social situation. I just take a deep breath, collect myself, and then go into that room full of people."

—a 45-year-old math teacher

"Your heart tells you to be with others, while simultaneously your head orders you to actively avoid them."

Reflections

Reflect on the following quote. Have you ever felt this way yourself? If so, how did you deal with it?

"Your heart tells you to be with others, while simultaneously your head orders you to actively avoid them."

_____

_____

_____

_____

_____

_____

_____

_____

_____

_____

_____

_____

_____

_____

_____

_____

DAY 5 The Slow-to-Warm-Up Tendency: Time to Adjust

What You Need to Know

An important dynamic of shyness and a key element to understanding the experience of shyness is the slow-to-warm-up tendency. Everybody needs time to warm up and adjust to new situations. If you are shy, however, you probably need more time than non-shy individuals to do so, particularly when trying to sort out the details of the approach-avoidance conflict.

Being slow to warm up is not a failing; it's just part of human nature. The heart of the problem—aside from your inclination to feel bad or inadequate about being slow—is not the actual slowness but rather the tendency for you and most other shy individuals to ignore this consequence of shyness and to rush through the warm-up period.

As a shy person, it is not uncommon for you to have unrealistic expectations of your ability to overcome slowness when warming up; for example, you probably often anticipate that you will "turn on" socially as soon as you walk into a party, or at least shortly afterward. When that doesn't happen, you then assume that you are less socially proficient than everyone else and quickly leave the social situation without giving yourself a fair amount of time to warm up.

By rushing through the warm-up period, you squander precious moments by focusing on negative feelings such as anxiety, self-doubt, and impending social disaster. In the process, you perpetuate the need to calculate how best to *avoid* others rather than how to *approach* them. Therefore, it is important for you to learn to understand and appreciate the slow-to-warm-up tendency so that you can make it work *for* you instead of *against* you. By fully comprehending this tendency, you will be able to view it as a critical step in learning to control your shyness.

Your Turn

Describe two or three situations in which you did not give yourself enough time to warm up—and the consequences for failing to do so.

1. _____

   _____

   _____

   _____

   _____

2. _____

   _____

   _____

   _____

   _____

3. _____

   _____

   _____

   _____

   _____

Voices

"I'm always perplexed about how I can show myself to be a decent guy—and as genuinely funny as I really am—when I meet someone. I don't get to be this way until I actually know somebody. Then I'm not concerned about saying what's on my mind or something completely nutty."

—a 35-year-old customer service representative

"I am often mistaken for or appear to be someone who is conceited, snobbish, and disinterested in others. This is not the case at all. When I take the time to talk to people one-on-one, they realize I am sensitive, caring, honest, and fun to be with. I am not sure why I am not confident in myself."

—a 20-something computer programmer

‘Being slow to warm up is not a failing; it's just part of human nature.’

Reflections

Do you agree or disagree with the statement below? If you disagree, do you think the reason is that your shyness is holding you back and preventing you from viewing your slow-to-warm-up tendency objectively?

"Being slow to warm up is not a failing; it's just part of human nature."

_____

_____

_____

_____

_____

_____

_____

_____

_____

_____

_____

_____

_____

_____

_____

DAY 6 Understanding the Comfort Zone: The Role of Routine

What You Need to Know

If you are shy, the comfort zone is the place you go when you need peace of mind and solace from the various pressures of daily life. Following are three examples of comfort zones that you create for yourself:

▶ A physical comfort zone in which you gravitate to places where you feel calm (e.g., your house or apartment)

▶ A social comfort zone in which you surround yourself with people you know well (e.g., your family and close friends)

▶ A personal comfort zone in which you engage in activities that you feel confident doing (e.g., cooking or talking about your favorite hobby)

These comfort zones are helpful to you because they are places that enable you to feel safe about thinking and behaving freely. They are places where you feel you can be yourself and not be shy.

Unfortunately, shyness tends to have the opposite effect by creating a stagnant, constricting, inflexible, or—in the worst case—shrinking comfort zone, which makes going to new places, trying new activities, or meeting new people difficult. Because you are shy, your comfort zones become hiding places where you can retreat when you feel anxious or overwhelmed. In a sense, therefore, your shyness becomes your comfort zone, forcing you to maintain your routine and avoid the risk of experiencing new situations and expanding your comfort zone. Becoming more aware of your comfort zone will help you implement strategies for controlling your shyness.

Your Turn

Describe your physical, social, and personal comfort zones and what social routines you have developed that serve to restrict the expansion of your comfort zone and promote your shyness.

Physical: _____

_____

_____

Social: _____

_____

_____

Personal: _____

_____

_____

Routines developed: _____

_____

_____

_____

_____

_____

_____

_____

Voices

"I'm really good one-on-one, especially if I know the other person well. In groups, forget it. I just don't feel comfortable. I've realized that the larger the group, the more I'm shy."

—a college sophomore

"I have found that as I get older and have more experiences, my shyness decreases. With a group of friends, especially those I've met on the Internet, I am quite outgoing and comfortable. Still, when I meet new people, or when I am required to give a presentation or speak to someone I don't know well who is in authority, I am extremely shy."

—a 30-year-old nurse's aide

"My social life is virtually nonexistent when I am not in a play. I cannot foster early friendships because I'm afraid of what these would-be friends will think if I call them. I am able to return calls but I can't make the first move. This bothers me but I haven't been able to do anything about it."

—a 28-year-old actress

'For shy individuals, their comfort zones become hiding places where they retreat when they feel anxious or overwhelmed.'

Reflections

Do you agree or disagree with the following statement? Why?

"For shy individuals, their comfort zones become hiding places where they retreat when they feel anxious or overwhelmed."

_____

_____

_____

_____

_____

_____

_____

_____

_____

_____

_____

_____

_____

_____

_____

DAY 7   Shyness and Self-Esteem: It's Not What You Think

What You Need to Know

Self-esteem is the evaluative component of the self-concept: how you feel about yourself.

Your global sense of self-esteem is how you feel about yourself in general, whereas the specific dimensions of your self-esteem include how you feel about certain aspects of yourself.

The relationship you create between your shyness and self-esteem becomes problematic when you feel negative about yourself in those specific areas of your life that are important to you but in which you feel uncertain or unfulfilled. For example, a shy individual may feel confident at a business meeting when talking with other professionals about a new product line because the discussion focuses on an area in which she feels confident (i.e., high self-esteem). However, she may feel uncertain about her ability to make conversation with individuals she does not know at a party (i.e., low self-esteem). In the latter case, her perceived lack of ability to engage in small talk makes it difficult for her to meet new people and try new activities; her difficulty in communicating in this environment is particularly exasperating because this is precisely the area of her personal life that is unfulfilled.

Your Turn

Describe what you consider to be your unique strengths and weaknesses. How do you think they relate to your shyness?

_____

_____

_____

_____

_____

_____

_____

_____

_____

_____

_____

_____

_____

_____

_____

_____

_____

Voices

"My shyness is expressed by not saying how I really feel because I'm afraid of rejection. I also avoid calling or writing people back because I'm not sure what to say, and if I do say things, then I won't have a lot to say. I feel that I'll somehow be rejected if I ever ask to get together with someone. I become jealous a lot because I wonder why I can't be like another person. I feel as if I'm worthless in my social aspects because I can't always talk about 'fun' stuff."

—a 19-year-old waitress

"I believe that my shyness can be changed if it becomes important enough for me to change. That isn't to say that I don't want to change it. Overall I'm glad that I'm making progress in that area."

—a 27-year-old graduate student

"What I have done to overcome shyness is try to overcome my low self-esteem. I have tried to learn to accept myself for who I am. I have also learned, through maturity, that others will also have to accept me for me. If they are bothered by my shyness, that's their problem."

—a 32-year-old mortgage broker

"A perceived lack of ability to engage in small talk makes it difficult to meet new people and try new activities."

Reflections

Does the following statement apply to you? Do you agree with its premise?

"A perceived lack of ability to engage in small talk makes it difficult to meet new people and try new activities."

_____

_____

_____

_____

_____

_____

_____

_____

_____

_____

_____

_____

_____

_____

_____

_____

DAY 8 Assessing Your Shyness: What Makes You Shy?

What You Need to Know

As you gain a greater understanding of how you experience your shyness by discovering what shyness is and is not, you should develop an appreciation for the three fundamental dynamics of shyness:

► The approach-avoidance conflict

► The slow-to-warm-up tendency

► The comfort zone

By keeping these three principles in mind and viewing the role of self-esteem in its proper context, you can enhance your understanding of your shyness by assessing what makes you feel shy. You can assess what makes you feel shy by thinking about when and where you feel shy, how your shyness makes you feel, and what you try to do about your shyness. To assist you in the systematic assessment of your shyness, complete the Personal Shyness Inventory on the following page.

Your Turn

Personal Shyness Inventory

Answer the following prompts or questions as completely as you can.

1. Describe factors you believe have contributed to your shyness.

   _____

   _____

   _____

2. Describe how your shyness is expressed.

   _____

   _____

   _____

3. Describe the problems your shyness has created in your life.

   _____

   _____

   _____

4. Describe what you have done to overcome your shyness.

   _____

   _____

   _____

5. What is there about your shyness that you would like to know more about?

   _____

   _____

   _____

Voices

"My shyness is expressed daily. I fear groups and talking in front of others, so I try to be nice to everyone so they'll think I'm a nice guy."

—a 45-year-old salesman

"I get nervous easily. If I have to go to the store, I hurry and do it as fast as I can. When I'm there, I don't look at other people, or I go really early when nobody's there. If I get stuck in line with other people, it's like I almost have a panic attack while I'm waiting and I've just got to hurry up and get out of there."

—a 30-something stay-at-home mom

'You can enhance your understanding of your shyness by determining what makes you feel shy.'

Reflections

Read the statement below and then jot down your assessment of your shyness.

"You can enhance your understanding of your shyness by determining what makes you feel shy."

_____

_____

_____

_____

_____

_____

_____

_____

_____

_____

_____

_____

_____

_____

_____

_____

_____

DAY 9 Becoming Successfully Shy: Taking Control of Your Shyness

What You Need to Know

Becoming successfully shy is not about changing who you are—after all, there's nothing wrong with being shy. In actuality, it involves the following:

▶ Being aware of and understanding the nature and basic dynamics of your shyness and incorporating this insight into your everyday living experiences

▶ Using the knowledge you've acquired to help you control your shyness rather than letting your shyness control you

▶ Expanding your comfort zone so you can achieve the goals that your shyness had previously prevented you from attaining

Your Turn

List a few of the goals you hope to achieve as you become successfully shy.

1. _____

_____

_____

2. _____

_____

_____

3. _____

_____

_____

4. _____

_____

_____

5. _____

_____

_____

Voices

"I do not want my shyness to cause me to experience life to a lesser degree. In large measure I have succeeded but recognize that it's a constant battle. My goal is not to battle it, but to accept it and exploit it for my best possible life experience. I can say that at age 53 fairly easily. For me, it would have been impossible at age 13 or 23. If I could have, life would have been that much fuller."

—a gym manager in the Midwest

"After a 25-year interruption of my studies I returned to school, and the first class I took was a speech class. Needless to say I was very frightened—not only by the class, but also by the fear of not being able to cope with the studies, my family, and work life. My professor taught me that no goal is impossible once one is clearly focused. I will always be grateful for his encouragement. Education has opened doors to worlds I only visited in my dreams."

—a 55-year-old social worker

‘Being successfully shy is about controlling your shyness instead of letting it control you.’

Reflections

Thus far, what—if anything—have you been thinking about and doing to enable yourself to become successfully shy? Use the following quote as a starting point.

"Being successfully shy is about using this knowledge to control your shyness instead of letting your shyness control you."

_____

_____

_____

_____

_____

_____

_____

_____

_____

_____

_____

_____

_____

_____

DAY 10 Making the Right Decisions: The Key to Your Success

What You Need to Know

As noted previously, if you are to become successfully shy, you must make changes in your life that reflect a personal sense of control over your shyness. Although change is not easy, you can decrease the difficulty associated with change by making decisions that are right for you. To help you make better decisions, you need to become aware of the Four I's and their roles in helping you to become successfully shy:

► Identification
► Information
► Incorporation
► Implementation

Identification—recognizing what you consider to be a problem associated with your shyness; the more specific you can be about the problem, the better (e.g., "I want to be able to approach and initiate a conversation with people I'm attracted to at social gatherings")

Information—obtaining the knowledge necessary for you to develop the strategies to address the problem, which is what you're doing as you read this workbook.

Incorporation—combining information and strategies so that they give you a better sense of your self and what that self is able to do

Implementation—using the information and strategies you have acquired to control your shyness

Using the decision-making approach described here to make changes in your life is an excellent way to gain control over your shyness. It makes it possible for you to systematically select those goals you hope to achieve and develop specific strategies for achieving these goals.

Your Turn

Select a problem related to your shyness and analyze it using the decision-making process associated with the Four I's. Repeat this exercise for several other problems related to your shyness.

_____

_____

_____

_____

_____

_____

_____

_____

_____

_____

_____

_____

_____

_____

_____

_____

_____

_____

Voices

"It's funny, but I know what the problem is, so I just have to do it. I don't think anyone could help me do that. Now I make more of an effort to talk to somebody. But sometimes I talk too fast and it doesn't make any sense, so I try to talk slower. I'm just trying so hard to talk and make conversation that I do it too fast. I think just relaxing would help a lot, too."

—a 27-year-old baker

"I have been trying to apply some new techniques to reduce and overcome shyness. These techniques include relaxation of muscle groups to relieve tension, slow breathing exercises, and forming positive statements about situations that provoke negative feelings and emotions. Also, I try to make light conversation with strangers in public places (e.g., a cashier at a store), and I use my bank lobby as opposed to an ATM."

—a 30-year-old jewelry designer

To help you make better decisions, you need to become aware of the Four I's: Identification, Information, Incorporation, and Implementation.

Reflections

Review the Four I's (listed below) and the roles they play in helping you to become successfully shy.

The Four I's: Identification, Information, Incorporation, Implementation.

Identificiation: _____

_____

_____

_____

Information: _____

_____

_____

_____

Incorporation: _____

_____

_____

_____

Implementation: _____

_____

_____

_____

DAY 11   Defining Shyness of the Mind: The Most Critical Component

What You Need to Know

Although you may believe your thoughts are unique, when it comes to your thoughts about shyness, you have much in common with most other shy individuals.

Shyness of the mind refers to the characteristic patterns of thinking shared by shy individuals. These patterns of thinking are based on myths and misinformation about shyness. Therefore, shy minds think about and respond to social situations in a manner that works against their best interests. On the other hand, shy minds are also powerful enough to break through this pattern.

It's possible for shy individuals to establish the truth about themselves and gain control of their shyness. All it takes is understanding the thought patterns of the shy mind and the determination to reconfigure them during social encounters.

Although there's a lot more to changing the shy mind than merely thinking positive thoughts, it's not as difficult as it may first appear. To help make this task easier, you must first break down the entrenched patterns into manageable parts and recognize the progression of these shy thoughts.

Your Turn

Examine your thought patterns carefully so you can recognize them and understand why they occur. Describe how what you think and believe about your shyness influences your behavior in specific social situations.

_____

_____

_____

_____

_____

_____

_____

_____

_____

_____

_____

_____

_____

_____

_____

_____

_____

Voices

"I have come to accept that strangers were just as nervous about me as I was about them, and there was no need to be afraid of them, as we were all in the same boat, really, and needed to get to know each other before judging. That was about four years ago. Now, I rarely have a problem, although I still don't walk up to strangers and speak as if I'd known them forever. But I do speak to them!"

—a 40-year-old seamstress

"I am often outgoing and friendly, but if I feel someone is watching me or judging me (whether or not they are in reality), I become exceedingly self-conscious. I can't eat if I feel someone is watching me. I feel as if I walk funny when people are watching me walk by (such as when I walk past a restaurant and I know people are watching me). I know this is incredibly stupid and narcissistic, but knowing that doesn't stop the behaviors."

—a 25-year-old data analyst

❝It's possible for shy individuals to establish the truth about themselves and gain control of their shyness.❞

Reflections

Do you agree or disagree with the following statement? Explain your reasoning.

"It's possible for shy individuals to establish the truth about themselves and gain control of their shyness."

_____

_____

_____

_____

_____

_____

_____

_____

_____

_____

_____

_____

_____

_____

_____

DAY 12 Understanding the Role of Anxiety: A Misunderstood Emotion

What You Need to Know

Anxiety is the emotion probably most often associated with shyness. Butterflies in the stomach, sweaty palms, tense muscles, dry mouth, and jittery speech in response to threatening social situations are all examples of how people typically report the symptoms of anxiety.

In reality, anxiety originates in the decision—based on previous experience or some real or imagined danger—to view a situation as threatening. Once alerted to the threat, individuals who are not shy are willing and able to prepare for it. From their perspective, therefore, anxiety enhances their ability to cope with a threat.

The emotion of anxiety acts differently on people with shy minds. For those individuals, anxiety detracts from their ability to deal effectively with threatening social situations. The reason is that people with shy minds are so busy concentrating on the emotion of anxiety that they have difficulty focusing on strategies they could develop and execute to cope with the threatening situation. As a result, it is difficult for shy individuals to perform successfully in these situations. To make matters worse, once they become aware that they are not developing or using any effective strategies, shy individuals become even more anxious, thus beginning a vicious cycle that further deflates them and causes them more anxiety.

Your Turn

Think of situations related to your shyness that create anxiety for you. Select three of those situations and describe how your anxiety interferes with your ability to respond successfully in those situations.

1. _____

_____

_____

_____

_____

_____

2. _____

_____

_____

_____

_____

_____

3. _____

_____

_____

_____

_____

_____

Voices

"I avoid things when possible. When I can't, I get a nervous feeling—a scared, wanting-to-run-away feeling; a feeling of being intensely scrutinized, as if people can see right into me; a feeling that if I open up, people will not like me, so why try; a feeling of fear and an inability to speak in front of a group of people, with sweating, an increased pounding heartbeat, blushing, and so on. I feel afraid, and at the same time I know how silly it is, but I can't control the feeling of fear that I feel."

—a 50-year-old nursing home attendant

"I get really stressed out when I talk to someone, even if it is just small talk. After I talk to the person, I realize I have broken out into a sweat, and I start going over everything I've said, in my mind, to see if I have said anything the person wouldn't like. If I think I did say something wrong, I start to feel bad."

—a 32-year-old human resources manager

‘In the shy mind, anxiety detracts from the ability to deal effectively with perceived threatening social situations.’

Reflections

Why do you think the following statement is true? How does anxiety work in the minds of individuals who are not shy?

"Anxiety works differently in the shy mind. In the shy mind, anxiety detracts from the ability to deal effectively with perceived threatening social situations."

_____

_____

_____

_____

_____

_____

_____

_____

_____

_____

_____

_____

_____

_____

DAY 13   Strategies for Controlling Your Anxiety: The Anxiety Advantage

What You Need to Know

Far from being detrimental, a certain degree of anxiety is beneficial. It means you are expanding your comfort zone and learning new life lessons. Without tension in your life, there would be no personal growth.

The key is controlling the degree of your anxiety and learning to use it to your advantage. To do so, you must first reframe your anxiety. For example, instead of thinking of yourself as anxious, think of yourself as someone in the midst of a heightened state of arousal. The way you feel is simply a natural part of what and how you should feel as you take new risks to expand your comfort zone, such as meeting new people or visiting different places.

Keep in mind that you must be realistic about your level of anxiety. For example, are you feeling truly overwhelmed and out of control, or is your anxiety less intense than that? Anything short of a full-blown panic attack is tolerable and controllable.

Allow the slow-to-warm-up tendency to run its course. For example, don't be too quick to turn and run from a social situation because you feel nervous shortly after arriving; such feelings are natural. In addition, learn from your anxiety by identifying the reason for it, and remember to focus on the task at hand—not your anxiety.

Finally, a general rule for controlling your anxiety is to be persistent. By learning new behaviors and repeating them, you will find that they become second nature to you; as a result, you will become less anxious over time. Don't give up. To be successfully shy, you must learn to tolerate situations that make you a little nervous. A good way to build tolerance is to take incremental courses of action and to view your anxiety as a source of growth.

Your Turn

Select three situations that create anxiety for you, and then describe what strategies you would use to control your anxiety in each of these situations.

Situations	**Strategies**
1. _____	_____
_____	_____
_____	_____
_____	_____
_____	_____
2. _____	_____
_____	_____
_____	_____
_____	_____
_____	_____
3. _____	_____
_____	_____
_____	_____
_____	_____
_____	_____

Voices

"Although at times I feel like I want to be more outgoing, I sometimes feel that being shy is advantageous. Many co-workers tell everything about their lives, and I feel that they are judged and talked about because of this."

—a 31-year-old doctor's assistant

"Socially, I sometimes freeze up. I'm easily intimidated. However, sometimes I think people may mistake my nervousness for enthusiasm, perhaps because I try so hard for it to seem this way. Furthermore, I'm pretty thin (My metabolism works like crazy!), and people say that I'm hyper, but I know I'm covering up major insecurities. I also imitate my mother in social situations—she's very animated and humorous."

—a 22-year-old supermarket clerk

"I think it is a desensitizing process. Working through what you are afraid of and having a successful experience eliminate the fear and anxiety."

—a 35-year-old postal carrier

‘The key is controlling the degree of your anxiety and learning to use it to your advantage.’

Reflections

Read the following quote. Can you explain, in general terms, how this process works?

"The key is controlling the degree of your anxiety and learning to use it to your advantage."

_____

_____

_____

_____

_____

_____

_____

_____

_____

_____

_____

_____

_____

_____

DAY 14 Narcissism and Selective Attention Deficit: The Problem with Excessive Self-Consciousness

What You Need to Know

It may be counterintuitive to conceive of shy people as narcissistic. After all, most people think of narcissists as individuals who are not shy and who seek attention—whose patterns of behavior do not include shyness.

The truth is that shy people are narcissistic, too; their shy minds are perfectly capable of creating a sense of narcissism in them. These shy individuals are so self-conscious that, like narcissists who are not shy, they see themselves as the center of attention: During their social interactions, most shy individuals feel that everybody is watching every move they make and evaluating everything they say. Of course, this notion is fallacious because most people are more concerned about their own social performance than that of others.

Shy individuals also experience a form of selective attention deficit. This pattern of thinking involves shy individuals' systematically focusing more on what they feel they are doing wrong than what they are doing right. For example, shy individuals are apt to focus on a single mistake they made during a conversation and at the same time disregard all the successful comments they made during that same conversation.

The main reason for this selective attention is that mistakes occur relatively infrequently and therefore are bound to be more noticeable than behavior or comments that are correct or error free; in other words, appropriate behavior and comments tend to become routine and consequently draw less attention. Because mistakes don't happen as often, they are more conspicuous. Excessive self-consciousness creates a tendency toward critical self-evaluation.

Your Turn

Describe a situation in which your shyness promoted a sense of narcissistic thinking caused by selective attention deficit.

_____

_____

_____

_____

_____

_____

_____

_____

_____

_____

_____

_____

_____

_____

_____

_____

_____

Voices

"What a curse! To be so consistently self-centered and fearful! 'How am I being perceived?' is the question that is uppermost in my mind—almost every waking moment. I'm very physically attractive (I'm constantly told) and fit; I'm also successful professionally. What a terrible shame that I can't enjoy it!"

—a 32-year-old saleswoman

"Being shy is being uncomfortable from the moment you realize you are going to be in a new environment with new people. You are consumed with what to wear. Will I be overdressed? Will I be underdressed? Will the quality of my clothes be good enough? Will I be able to carry on an intelligent conversation? And above all, what if they don't like me? The degree of discomfort is directly related to how important the impression you make on these people will be."

—a 46-year-old florist

‘Most people are more concerned with their own social performance than that of others.’

Reflections

Do you find that the following statement almost always holds true?

"Most people are more concerned with their own social performance than that of others."

_____

_____

_____

_____

_____

_____

_____

_____

_____

_____

_____

_____

_____

_____

_____

_____

DAY 15 Controlling Excessive Self-Consciousness: Promoting Realistic Self-Evaluations

What You Need to Know

For you, the shy person, and for most everyone else as well, a certain degree of self-consciousness is a natural component of your interactions with others: It's what keeps you connected to others in social situations.

The main problem you have with self-consciousness is that it begins to override the natural expression of your personality, causing you to make adjustments. Once you learn how to adjust and how to control your self-consciousness, you will be well on your way to becoming successfully shy.

To counteract the excessive self-consciousness that your shyness amplifies, it is helpful for you to rethink the nature of your critical self-evaluation and focus on expressing yourself more naturally. Here are some steps you can follow that should enable you to do so. (Note: Remain calm during this period of adjustment. Remember that your initial sense of self-consciousness is part of the warm-up period.)

1. Reflect on your current typical response. Then recall that you have other responses at your disposal besides being self-conscious, such as offering a simple greeting, paying a compliment, or focusing on what others are saying.

2. Now that you have given some thought to other potential responses, think of your self-consciousness as something that would naturally be your first response. The same holds true for others. If you keep that in mind, then you should be able to remain calm.

3. After the initial experience of self-consciousness, move on to the next response, which might be a comment intended to help keep the conversation going—for example, "How do you know the host?" or "Tell me about your interesting lapel pin."

4. Understand the roles of accentuation and exaggeration. Realize that an act of yours that you may be focusing on and blowing out of proportion (e.g., your perception of a brief

pause before your response to a question as a giant lull in the conversation) is not as apparent to others as it seems to you.

5. Confront your sense of self-consciousness directly. A good idea is to practice your responses as you stand in front of a mirror. Another good idea is to tape-record your responses and then listen to how you sound when you play back the tape.

Your Turn

1. Think of an occasion when you felt excessively self-conscious. Describe which strategies you used to deal with the situation.

_____

_____

_____

_____

_____

_____

2. Think of a situation that you have yet to encounter but may in the near future. Which strategies do you think you might use to alleviate your self-consciousness?

_____

_____

_____

_____

_____

_____

Voices

"When I realized that the kids in my high school were ridiculous for teasing me, I gained a lot of confidence. It was like a huge weight lifted off of me because I could look at the situation in a different light."

—a college freshman

"I take a good look at myself and tell myself that I have no reason to feel insecure and I can't let other people decide my life. They have no control over me and what I do. I force myself to be with others and then I feel better."

—a 25-year-old fashion buyer

❝The problem shy individuals have with self-consciousness is that it begins to override the natural expression of their personalities.❞

Reflections

Have you had problems with self-consciousness, as described in the following statement?

"The problem shy individuals have with self-consciousness is that it begins to override the natural expression of their personalities."

_____

_____

_____

_____

_____

_____

_____

_____

_____

_____

_____

_____

_____

DAY 16 Explaining Attributional Process: Playing the Blame Game

What You Need to Know

Attributions are used by all of us, shy or not, to create explanations for our actions and the actions of others. The attributional process helps us render life more predictable, orderly, secure, and reasonable by explaining seemingly random events. In your case, as in others, it probably plays out like this:

In general, you attribute events to three categories of causes and use these rationales—in various combinations—to explain any occurrence, be it a car crash, a forest fire, or even a social snub.

> The first category includes either internal attributions, where you assume the cause is within your realm of responsibility, or external attributions, where you assume the cause is outside your realm of responsibility.

> The second category includes stable attributions, where the cause may be something permanent, or unstable attributions, where the cause is something temporary or easily changed.

> The third category includes specific attributions, where cause is related to a particular situation, or global attributions, where the cause is something that will occur in every situation.

Because the nature of the attributional explanations you propose can give you hope ("Things will be better with the next person I approach") or take hope away ("No matter what I say, people will reject me"), it is important to understand the operation of the attributional process.

Your Turn

Has this notion of attributional explanations given you hope?
Has it taken away hope? Explain.

_____

_____

_____

_____

_____

_____

_____

_____

_____

_____

_____

_____

_____

_____

_____

_____

Voices

"I have begun to dread lunches with the people I work with because when I go to them I get really nervous. Then I start talking too much and it makes me feel really awkward. I try to think up something funny to say but I can't and I end up leaving the lunch feeling bad, feeling no one likes me because I was a blabbermouth and that it was all my fault."

—a 23-year-old administrative assistant

"In some instances, I become nervous when I think that I am going to run out of things to say. I'll just blurt out anything to try and keep the conversation going. Then I look at the conversation in hindsight, and regret what I have said, because I usually feel like it made me look completely incompetent or just plain stupid. Sometimes in my mind, while I am talking, I just keep thinking, 'Shut up! You're making a fool of yourself!'"

—a 26-year-old photo editor

'The attributional process helps us render life more predictable, orderly, secure, and reasonable by explaining seemingly random events.'

Reflections

Can you come up with a few examples that underscore the importance of the attributional process described in the following quote?

"The attributional process helps us render life more predictable, orderly, secure, and reasonable by explaining seemingly random events."

1. _____

_____

_____

_____

_____

2. _____

_____

_____

_____

_____

3. _____

_____

_____

_____

_____

DAY 17 Common Attributional Errors: Losing the Blame Game

What You Need to Know

Although there are many possible combinations of attributions that can be made, the pattern of attributions made by shy individuals for their actions tends to be biased and works against them. The reason is that shy individuals tend to overemphasize internal, stable, and global attributions for their social failures. For example, if a shy individual has difficulty talking with someone at a party, the pattern of causal explanation is that he is boring that person (internal attribution), that he will bore other individuals at this party (stable attribution), and that he will probably bore people in all social interactions (global attribution).

A pattern of attributions such as this is referred to as the "pessimistic attributional style," and it effectively destroys self-confidence. This pattern shows that it is impossible to be self-assured when you believe that you, and only you, cause foul-ups.

On the other hand, shy individuals tend to overemphasize external, unstable, and specific attributions for their social successes. For example, if you are the shy person who happens to have a successful conversation at a party, you will assume that it was just luck (external attribution) that you found the only person at the party patient and kind enough to talk to you; that your conversational skills were unusually good that day (unstable attribution); and that a similar set of circumstances (specific attribution) is not likely to happen again. It is easy to see how this kind of attribution pattern tends to undermine any sense of personal achievement that comes with success; it can also erode self-confidence.

Your Turn

Describe some of the attributional errors you have made to explain your actions. Also illustrate the situations in which they occurred.

_____

_____

_____

_____

_____

_____

_____

_____

_____

_____

_____

_____

_____

_____

_____

_____

Voices

"Overcoming shyness has been something I wish I did not have to deal with, but I do. I have tried to tell myself that I am harder on me than anyone else will ever be, and that I should just forget it. Maybe my problem isn't shyness. Maybe it's self-confidence and/or self-concept. But I hate myself and I hate what my shyness has made me. I think the way I see my shyness is a bit warped because I know my friends are a bit overconfident. So I see myself as a little bit more abnormal than I am. Also, if I don't know how a person will react to something (like me going up to them) I won't try it."

—a high school senior

"I always feel rejected because I do not have any great value to anybody and seem stupid. Especially in a gathering of a group of strangers. I do not want to make a fool of myself nor do I wish to make a nuisance of myself where I feel I am not wanted or accepted. So I generally wait until someone speaks to me."

—a 58-year-old small-business owner

Shy individuals tend to overemphasize internal, stable, and global attributions for their social failures.

Reflections

Being shy, you are no doubt familiar with the message in the following statement. Give an example of an occasion on which you overemphasized attributions for a social failure.

"Shy individuals tend to overemphasize internal, stable, and global attributions for their social failures."

_____

_____

_____

_____

_____

_____

_____

_____

_____

_____

_____

_____

_____

DAY 18   Controlling Attributional Errors: Playing the Blame Game Fairly

What You Need to Know

With an understanding of the attributional biases associated with the shy mind, you can begin to seek out other thought patterns that are less biased, more fair, and promote a greater sense of self-confidence. Try using the following examples:

1. Practice external/unstable/specific attributions when things are going poorly.

   Example: When you are having difficulty speaking with someone at a social function, it's possible that, just like you, this person is shy and might also have trouble making conversation, or that having trouble conversing with this person does not mean you will have trouble conversing with others.

2. Practice internal/stable/global attributions when things are going well.

   Example: When you are carrying on a successful conversation at a social function, take some personal credit for the success by assuming it has something to do with some skills you possess that will carry over into your interactions with other individuals in future situations.

3. Remind yourself that "everybody else feels this way."

   Example: It's helpful to remind yourself that almost everyone feels uncomfortable when making a speech in front of a large group of individuals, being introduced to someone in a position of authority or someone to whom you are attracted, or meeting new people in a new situation. Nobody is perfect, so don't feel you have to be.

4. Be realistic and fair with your attributions.

   Example: Just as it is unfair to blame yourself always and assume all of the responsibility for your social failures, so is it unreasonable never to assume responsibility and always to blame others for your social failures.

By temporarily withholding judgment and being able to take a more systematic look at your attributions, you will be in a much better position to be fair to yourself and to others. You will eventually learn to accept your social successes and acquire a sense of hope that will make it possible to alter those thoughts and actions that seem to contribute to your social failures.

Your Turn

Reanalyze those situations in which you have made attributional errors, and then follow up by employing more realistic attributional strategies.

_____

_____

_____

_____

_____

_____

_____

_____

_____

_____

_____

_____

_____

_____

_____

_____

_____

Voices

"I have read everything I could find on shyness. I have tried adjusting my thinking as much as I could, and though I can now take what people say and do less personally, which helps a great deal with the job I have, I still find most social situations terrifying, and even social chitchat difficult."

—a 31-year-old CPA

"By making a conscious mental footnote that I am an equal with my employer, I have begun to adjust and balance my inner shyness toward him. When I say 'equal,' I mean equal on a humanistic level, for I am not an equal on the professional level."

—a 33-year-old mechanic

'Nobody is perfect, so don't feel you have to be.'

Reflections

Regarding the following quote, have you found this problem to be prevalent in your life and difficult to overcome?

"Nobody is perfect, so don't feel you have to be."

_____

_____

_____

_____

_____

_____

_____

_____

_____

_____

_____

_____

_____

_____

_____

_____

DAY 19 Common Social Comparison Errors: When Uncertainty Promotes Unfairness

What You Need to Know

Comparing yourself to others is a natural and useful tendency. Such social comparisons help you to determine how to act, what to discuss, and where to stand—in short, how to integrate into society. Social comparisons can be especially helpful when you are in new or uncertain situations: Turning to see what others are doing can be a source of much relief in such novel situations. Unfortunately, shy individuals—burdened by a shy mind—will tend to compare themselves unfairly and unfavorably to others and, as a result, constantly feel inferior.

When you compare yourself to the center of attention—the speaker at the podium, the life of the party, the celebrity at the premiere—rather than to the other members of the audience or other quiet people at the party, you can't help but feel inferior. As a shy person, your sense of uncertainty about your social abilities, along with the corresponding sense of distress it creates, will increase the likelihood that social comparisons will be a dominant mental activity of yours and that you will tend to compare yourself to the most salient features of the social situation.

Caught in the trap of such unfair social comparisons, your confidence will weaken and your sense of esteem will decline. As a result, there will be less likelihood of your taking any type of action other than silence, avoidance, or withdrawal.

Your Turn

Describe how your feelings of uncertainty in specific social situations have resulted in your making unfair social comparisons between yourself and others, and discuss the consequences of these unfair comparisons.

_____

_____

_____

_____

_____

_____

_____

_____

_____

_____

_____

_____

_____

_____

_____

_____

Voices

"I've always been well involved socially, but I tend to become shy around different or unfamiliar people so I can see how they behave first. Sometimes I become shy if I am afraid rejection is involved."

—a 19-year-old telemarketer

"As I see people around me surrounded by their groups of friends, I feel almost abnormal, as I do not have a group of close friends. This leads to an almost constant feeling that I am missing out on life because I am not able to share these experiences. This is especially apparent when I see groups of people at public places (i.e., a bar) enjoying each other's company while laughing and having a good time. I am constantly very self-conscious and worried about others' passing judgment on me."

—a 35-year-old fashion buyer

"Shy individuals tend to compare themselves unfairly and unfavorably to others and, as a result, constantly feel inferior."

Reflections

As a shy person, do you notice that you habitually compare your-self unfairly and unfavorably to individuals who are popular or often in the limelight? Do you agree with the following statement?

"Shy individuals tend to compare themselves unfairly and unfavorably to others and, as a result, constantly feel inferior."

_____

_____

_____

_____

_____

_____

_____

_____

_____

_____

_____

_____

_____

_____

_____

DAY 20 Controlling Unfair Social Comparisons: Promoting Self-Confidence with Fair Comparisons

What You Need to Know

Controlling the consequences of unfair social comparisons involves making social comparisons that promote a sense of self-confidence rather than detract from it. To do so, you must first decide which qualities are worth comparing. Because comparisons ultimately affect self-esteem, you should compare only those aspects of your personality that matter to you. You should also try to do the following:

Compare yourself with people who are more like you than unlike you.

Make social comparisons with those who share similar experiences with you.

Use your upward social comparisons (i.e., your comparisons with people who are outgoing) to gain knowledge. If you find that you're comparing yourself to socially successful individuals, do so with an eye to learning what makes them so good at what they do. What, for example, can they teach you about the following?

When they are involved in a conversation, do socially successful people try to expand on the comments made by others and make a special effort to let others express their opinions?

Are they polite and complimentary to others?

Do they know how to tell jokes and make people laugh?

When they are at a party, do they feel comfortable looking for someone nice and attractive they'd like to have as a dance partner?

If you follow these pointers, rather than feeling bad about your inadequacies, you can learn from your contacts with socially successful people. You will also discover that the key to controlling unfair social comparisons is to be realistic and fair in the comparisons you make of yourself to others.

Your Turn

Using your knowledge of social comparisons, reanalyze those situations that previously prompted unfair comparisons by discussing strategies you have employed that make possible social comparisons of yourself that are fair.

_____

_____

_____

_____

_____

_____

_____

_____

_____

_____

_____

_____

_____

_____

_____

_____

Voices

"Basically I try to tell myself the same thing every time I feel my shyness is going to interfere with something I am doing or alter the impression I am going make on someone. I just try to convince myself that while fear is legitimate, you can help yourself to control your reactions to it by understanding what is going on in your head. I tell myself that nothing is going to be the end of the world and that confidence looks so much better than fear. I also tell myself that I am not stupid, and if I don't speak up, people will never know what I am all about, and I am leaving it up to them to draw their own conclusions about me. I should actually be controlling how I would like people to view me. I am, after all, the master of my own destiny."

—a 24-year-old veterinary assistant

"Since comparisons ultimately affect self-esteem, compare only those aspects of your personality that matter to you."

Reflections

Have you been able to adhere to the advice given in the following statement?

"Since comparisons ultimately affect self-esteem, compare only those aspects of your personality that matter to you."

_____

_____

_____

_____

_____

_____

_____

_____

_____

_____

_____

_____

_____

_____

_____

_____

_____

DAY 21 **Expanding Your Comfort Zone: Gently Widening Your Range of Experiences**

What You Need to Know

The key to expanding your comfort zone is to break out of your routine. Your strategy, however, should be to widen your range of experiences in a down-to-earth fashion rather than pretend you are a confident, outgoing, seemingly fearless adventurer.

Slowly but steadily, you should begin participating in a range of new activities, many of which once made you uncomfortable. Your goal should be to expand your comfort zone by increasing the frequency of your approaches to less familiar situations, surroundings, and people while at the same time strengthening your emotional and psychological resources. The following suggestions should help you in your efforts to expand your comfort zone:

▶ Build on what you already feel sure about.

▶ Add variations to routine activities.

▶ Step out in public more often.

If it will make you feel more comfortable, invite a friend to join you in taking part in these new activities.

Regardless of whether you are alone or with a friend, you should make an effort to broaden your interests. For example, if you enjoy particular kinds of music, art, or theater, then you should go to concerts, exhibits, and performances that feature your favorite styles. If you like jogging or tennis, you should join a community runners' group or tennis league. You might even consider extending your interests to other forms of athletic activities, such as canoeing or hiking. In addition, any hobbies or leisure activities that you enjoy might help you meet others who share the same interests; perhaps you could join local groups.

While seeking opportunities to expand your comfort zone, it is important that you keep your expectations realistic. For example, you may have to repeat many of these activities before you feel comfortable with them, just as you repeated many of the activities that make up your present comfort zone.

Your Turn

Select those areas of your comfort zone that you would like to expand, and describe how you would use the strategies presented in this workbook to do so. It is important to realize that the more specific you can be about which aspects of the comfort zone you desire to expand and your strategies for doing so, the easier it will be to implement the changes.

_____

_____

_____

_____

_____

_____

_____

_____

_____

_____

_____

_____

_____

_____

_____

_____

Voices

"My shyness has not seemed to have created a lot of problems that I am aware of. I do feel insecure when I meet someone new in my personal life. It takes me a long time to feel secure and open up, but I never quit trying. In my social life I tend to avoid large crowds, large cities, large parties, but I don't feel I am missing anything. In my professional life, shyness seems to disappear. I am a different person when I am giving my workshops."

—a 35-year-old aromatherapist

"I try to overcome my shyness a little each day by forcing myself to speak up when I am afraid. When I do muster up the courage to be myself in front of others, I experience a great peace with myself and a feeling of accomplishment. This is a hope for a better me."

—a 39-year-old banker

'Slowly but steadily, you can add new endeavors that once made you uncomfortable.'

Reflections

List some strategies that you think can help you become comfortable with new endeavors and make the following sentence come true.

"Slowly but steadily, you can add new endeavors that once made you uncomfortable."

1. _____

_____

_____

_____

_____

2. _____

_____

_____

_____

_____

3. _____

_____

_____

_____

_____

DAY 22 Performing Social Reconnaissance: Planning and Preparing for Your Social Success

What You Need to Know

Social reconnaissance involves gathering information about a social situation before you enter it. The primary purpose of social reconnaissance is to reduce the ambiguity, uncertainty, and anxiety often associated with meeting new people in new settings.

This takes some thought, focus, and preparation. For example, in addition to thinking about what you are going to wear to a social function, the practice of social reconnaissance would include your thinking about what you are going to talk about—and then rehearsing it.

Before you begin preparing, make sure you have something to say. Because shy individuals worry about not having anything to say, you can reduce your anxiety by developing a conversational knowledge base prior to the social event. Also before the event, you can visit other new social settings ahead of time. While on these preliminary visits, you can talk with some of the personnel from the establishments, learn from them, and listen to any pointers they can offer. Preliminary actions such as these will reduce your uncertainty and increase your confidence.

Next, familiarize yourself ahead of time with others whom you will be socializing with, and, while in the comfort of your home, rehearse what you are likely to say or do at the social gathering. For example, practice in front of a mirror: What will you do when you introduce yourself to others you will be meeting for the first time? How will you pronounce an artist's name or a foreign item on a menu? What will you add to a conversation about a particular news story in a conversation?

At this point, you may be thinking that planning and rehearsing for social interactions sounds a bit trite and artificial. The truth is quite the opposite: Getting over such logistical and initial conversational difficulties in advance of meeting new individuals in new settings will do much to put you at ease and allow you to focus on the real tasks at hand, which are making others feel comfortable, letting others get to know the real you, and enjoying yourself.

When you interact with individuals in social situations outside of your comfort zone, your shyness typically manifests itself in the form of behavior deficits. Because of this, the acquisition of new social and conversational skills is critical. And the best way for you to acquire and develop such skills is to define what information and skills you need, gather the information, and practice the skills ahead of time in a comfortable environment.

Your Turn

Describe how you would use social reconnaissance to help prepare yourself for various social situations you have had difficulty dealing with in the past. It is important to realize that the more specific you can be about what you have difficulty with and the actions in your plan of social reconnaissance, the easier it will be to implement the changes.

_____

_____

_____

_____

_____

_____

_____

_____

_____

_____

_____

_____

_____

_____

Voices

"As far as overcoming my shyness, there are times when I'll really try hard. I break things down into steps rather than making myself feel so overwhelmed. I would never get anything done then. One time I was answering an ad about a job and I was so nervous. I didn't worry about getting the job but concentrated on what I would say on the phone. So what I did was I thought about what the person I admire most would do. I gained the courage to make the call. I didn't get the job, but was happy I got past that first obstacle. Sometimes I'll turn down people's help, not to hurt them, but just to see if I can do something on my own. It works! I know that I have to take control because no one else will."

—a 22-year-old medical student

❛The best way for you to acquire and develop such skills is to define what information and skills you need, gather the information, and practice the skills ahead of time in a comfortable environment.❜

Reflections

What do you think of the following suggestion? Do you think it will be helpful to you?

"The best way for you to acquire and develop such skills is to define what information and skills you need, gather the information, and practice the skills ahead of time in a comfortable environment."

_____

_____

_____

_____

_____

_____

_____

_____

_____

_____

_____

_____

_____

_____

_____

DAY 23   **Taking Advantage of the Warm-Up Process: Actively Responding to the Passage of Time**

What You Need to Know

Instead of viewing the warm-up period as a time of drudgery, awkwardness, and excessive self-consciousness as a result of simply waiting for time to pass, you can use it to take action that will make it easier for you to interact with others once this period has passed. You can also use the time simply to relax before the event and to learn social etiquette.

One of the first things to keep in mind is to arrive early, not fashionably late. A common mistake is for shy individuals to show up late to a social function so that they can blend easily into the crowd that has already developed, thus feeling less self-conscious. The problem with this strategy is that it usually doesn't work: It is much more difficult to join groups of people that are already interacting than starting a conversation with someone on a one-to-one basis.

When you arrive late, you thus have two problems to deal with: the warm-up period and the difficulty of entering into preexisting groups. A more effective strategy is to arrive a little early so that you start your warm-up process before the social function begins. You'll have an opportunity to meet people as they arrive, and you can also ask the host or event coordinator if there is something you can do to help, such as pass out hors d'oeuvres.

Arriving early not only is polite and a good way for you to overcome your shyness, it also enables you to use the warm-up period to perform social reconnaissance. During this period, you should have ample time to familiarize yourself with the surroundings, to observe the décor, and to circulate among the other guests. As you do, you will notice certain things that people are wearing, such as rings, lapel pins, ties, blouses, or briefcases, which you can use later to initiate a conversation with these individuals when you feel more comfortable.

Also during the warm-up period, you might try employing the wait-and-hover technique. All you have to do is stand at the edge of different groups and listen to comments made by individuals that you can use as a starting point later on when you feel comfortable approaching specific individuals.

The warm-up period also gives you an opportunity to seek out like-minded people—those who, like you, seem quiet but still have plenty of interesting topics to talk about. Above all, you should be patient and never rush the warm-up process. You should realize that the length of the warm-up period differs from person to person.

Your Turn

Describe the actions you would take to deal with the specific situations you are likely to experience during the warm-up period. It is important to realize that the more specific you can be about the situations and the actions you are going to take, the easier it will be to implement the changes you desire.

_____

_____

_____

_____

_____

_____

_____

_____

_____

_____

_____

_____

_____

_____

_____

_____

Voices

"Being shy is not being able to remember someone's name when you are introduced to them and you are unprepared. For example, when you are out with a friend and they run into someone they know, they do the polite thing and introduce you. When this happens to me, because I'm not prepared, I didn't know I would be meeting someone and therefore I couldn't work myself up for it. All I can think about is what kind of impression I'm making. So, in turn, I have no idea what their name is."

—28-year-old TV production assistant

"I have tried several things to overcome my shyness. I have forced myself to go to clubs and parties, but I always chicken out when it comes to actually having to approach anyone. I psyche myself up to talk to people in my class, but always chicken out there too. I want to be able to be more open, but it's hard."

—a 24-year-old secretary and student

❛Arrive a little early so that you start your warm-up process before the social function begins. This will also give you the opportunity to meet people as they arrive.❜

Reflections

What do you think of the advice offered below? Do you feel that you are capable of succeeding with this strategy?

"Arrive a little early so that you start your warm-up process before the social function begins. This will also give you the opportunity to meet people as they arrive."

_____

_____

_____

_____

_____

_____

_____

_____

_____

_____

_____

_____

_____

_____

_____

_____

DAY 24 Preventing Self-Medication: Avoiding the Trap of Liquid Extroversion

What You Need to Know

Liquid extroversion refers to a strategy that involves shy individuals' consuming alcohol to help them feel more relaxed and less self-conscious during the initial stages of novel social situations. Although the consumption of alcohol may help individuals feel less self-conscious by giving them something to do with their hands, it is a strategy to be avoided.

The principal reason it should be avoided is that alcohol is classified as a depressant of the nervous system, which makes experiencing feelings of arousal and nervousness less likely. However, in addition to reducing the nervousness associated with the initial phase of the warm-up period, alcohol also interferes with those mental processes associated with performing successfully in social situations.

Another problem with the consumption of alcohol involves the attribution process. When you attribute your lack of tension and increased sociability to the consumption of alcohol, you conclude that the alcohol was responsible and assume that you can be relaxed and social only when drinking. However, such an attribution pattern fails to consider another important factor: the passage of time. In your case, the reduction in the degree of your nervousness could be attributed to your having remained in the situation for 35 minutes! By accepting personal responsibility for your willingness to remain in the situation throughout the initial period of adjustment, instead of assuming it was the alcohol that made you social (i.e., external attribution), you increase the likelihood that you will find the courage from within to remain in future novel situations during the warm-up period.

Your Turn

Describe some of the other physical, social, and personal draw-backs of employing the strategy of liquid extroversion to deal with shyness.

_____

_____

_____

_____

_____

_____

_____

_____

_____

_____

_____

_____

_____

_____

_____

_____

Voices

"I acted like a crazy man when I drank, and people seemed to enjoy me more. I got a reputation as being kind of crazy and wild when I did drink, so I showed a side of me that nobody really saw before."

—a 35-year-old computer programmer

"Returning to my hometown with a doctorate, I was kind of an important figure. Nevertheless, I continued finding refuge in alcohol for a social life and I had embarrassing situations with my wife, friends, and relatives, even with the community where I was a leader."

—a 59-year-old professor

"In social situations I will use alcohol moderately to loosen up, be less self-conscious and more outgoing. Nonetheless, I find it almost impossible to start a conversation with strangers, especially women. I cannot think of anything to talk about."

—a 42-year-old electrician

"Alcohol interferes with those mental processes associated with performing successfully in social situations."

Reflections

In your experience, has the following held true? Explain.

"Alcohol interferes with those mental processes associated with performing successfully in social situations."

_____

_____

_____

_____

_____

_____

_____

_____

_____

_____

_____

_____

_____

_____

_____

_____

DAY 25 Practicing Quick Talk: Setting the Stage for Conversational Contacts

What You Need to Know

Clearly, among the most difficult problems that shy individuals have is making the initial contact with others at social functions. At the heart of this difficulty seems to be the approach-avoidance conflict: Shy individuals want to approach others, but they avoid doing so for fear of not knowing how.

The key to increasing your ability to approach others is to use quick talk, which involves engaging others in conversation for only brief periods. The purpose of quick talk is to help you get used to talking to a variety of individuals at the same time these individuals get used to talking to you. When you practice quick talk, you must keep several things in mind:

1. It's more important to be nice than brilliant. Avoid putting undo pressure on yourself by feeling you have to be brilliant, urbane, or witty to capture the attention of others. All you really have to be is nice.

2. Begin the quick talk with comments about the shared environment, about the situation the two of you are in together. For example, a discussion about the shared environment might include a give-and-take about what you and the other individual have in common with respect to the immediate situation. The chat could involve anything from the weather to the unique features of the house you are visiting to the new movie theater in town to the upcoming concert and how much of a hassle it will be to buy tickets because of the inevitable crush of people in the long line.

3. Don't worry that some of your comments and small talk may sound trite because, after all, the purpose of such statements is to let the other individual know you are willing to talk—nothing more, nothing less. If the person responds with another comment about the shared environment, the purpose of such a statement is to show you that the other person is willing to talk with you, too.

4. Practice quick talk daily. You can use it in a variety of everyday situations—not just in more structured social situ-

ations—with people you meet while riding in an elevator, waiting in the checkout line, or examining an item of clothing at the mall.

5. Practice your quick talk with a variety of individuals. Acquiring this habit will help you to feel comfortable making conversation with all kinds of people. Soon others will know that you like to converse and will want to talk with you. Your willingness—actually eagerness—to talk will make you appear receptive and approachable to others.

6. Two more advantages of quick talk are that it can be used as a stepping-stone to more extended conversations with others in the future and can also reduce the risk associated with approaching others.

Your Turn

Describe a number of situations in which you will have the opportunity to practice quick talk and how you will do so. Keep in mind that the more specific you can be about the situations and the actions you are going to take, the easier it will be to implement the changes you wish to make.

1. _____

_____

_____

_____

2. _____

_____

_____

_____

3. _____

_____

_____

_____

4. _____

_____

_____

_____

Voices

"I have tried to overcome my shyness by having small conversations with anyone I may come into contact with, speaking up in meetings at work, going out to clubs with my fiancée, and focusing on relaxing when I become nervous."

—a 24-year-old executive assistant

"I was not taught that when you take a risk in a relationship, be it starting one or maintaining one, with a friend or a stranger, you will always be rewarded. The reward may pay off in improved people skills or increased confidence, both of which might prompt further risk. But the key is that there is always a reward for taking a risk. I learned this much later in life."

—a 47-year-old accountant

❛Shy individuals want to approach others but avoid doing so for fear of not knowing how.❜

Reflections

Do you feel confident that the pointers given in this workbook will enable you to conquer the approach-avoidance problem, as described below?

"Shy individuals want to approach others but avoid doing so for fear of not knowing how."

_____

_____

_____

_____

_____

_____

_____

_____

_____

_____

_____

_____

_____

_____

DAY 26   Taking Advantage of Rejection: Finding Useful Information

What You Need to Know

The old saying goes that you *should not* take rejection personally. I disagree. You *should* take rejection personally.

What you should never do, however, is to make rejection personal. In other words, don't take it as a personal affront. Don't take it as a criticism of your *self*—as a measure of the type of person you are. Taking rejection personally is based on something you did, such as how and when you introduced yourself. Making rejection personal, on the other hand, involves passing judgment on your sense of self, on the way you see yourself. The key to learning to accept rejection without feeling humbled or downcast is to keep rejection in the proper perspective.

Perhaps the best way to get a handle on the problem is to keep in mind that rejection is simply a part of life: Everybody experiences it. Anytime you take a risk or try something new or attempt to expand your comfort zone, there is the possibility of your facing rejection. This is not necessarily a negative outcome, though, because, in actuality, taking a risk and then either being rejected or failing is a natural part of growing up; it is part of the foundation of personal growth.

Another truth about rejection is that it is rare. Because of this, when rejection does occur, you are apt to give it more attention than it merits; you may even exhibit an intensely personal reaction owing to the high degree of personal attention that you give it. Furthermore, because you are generally accepted by others and are rarely rebuffed, any rejection stands out in your mind. You can reduce the pain of rejection by viewing it—among your experiences—as the exception to the rule, not the standard by which you judge your sense of self.

You should also recognize that your response to rejection is more important than your being rejected. There is nothing wrong with being rejected. The real concern is your reaction to the rejection. To help, instead of viewing rejection as a sign of failure, you should respond to rejection by developing strategies that will minimize the likelihood of such rejection occurring again. The key to developing your strategies is to gather information about what you have done in the past and what you should do differently in the future. To help in this regard, think of rejection as information in the form of feedback. Rejection should be considered as feedback to your actions, not a statement about you as a person. By regarding rejection as feedback, you can use it as information that can enhance your interactions with others. What's critical is how you react to the feedback and what you do with the information that the feedback provides.

Your Turn

Describe situations in which you have felt a sense of being rejected. Next, describe what feedback you received from these situations and the strategies you then developed to enhance your performance.

1. _____

_____

_____

_____

_____

_____

2. _____

_____

_____

_____

_____

_____

3. _____

_____

_____

_____

_____

_____

Voices

"Shyness causes a lot of inner pain and anguish. The worst part of it is a failure of the self to open up to friends and acquaintances. There is a strong fear of personal risk involved."

—a 46-year-old computer repair technician

"I think the root of shyness (mine, anyway) is the need for acceptance and approval. Plain and simple, that's all it is. It is the fear of rejection that keeps me quiet. Reject others before they reject you. It's supposed to hurt less that way. In the long run, does it really? I'm beginning to wonder."

—a 28-year-old translator

"I feel as if people will find out something awful about me if I expose myself to them. I know that I am a good person with no terrible, dark secret to hide, yet I battle with the feeling of hiding myself from others."

—a 40-something homemaker

"The key to learning to take rejection is to keep it in the proper perspective."

Reflections

How difficult is it to follow the advice given below?

"The key to learning to take rejection is to keep it in the proper perspective."

_____

_____

_____

_____

_____

_____

_____

_____

_____

_____

_____

_____

_____

_____

_____

_____

DAY 27 Focusing on Your Social Successes: Creating Opportunities for Personal Enhancement

What You Need to Know

Focusing on your social successes involves creating opportunities that will allow you to succeed and experience a sense of personal achievement. However, not all opportunities to succeed will pan out—especially those that are high risk. Taking high risks offers relatively little likelihood of success and, as a result, not much opportunity to experience a sense of personal achievement.

The key to creating opportunities that provide both a sense of success and personal achievement is to control the risks you take. The following pointers should prove helpful:

Take moderate risks. Moderate risks offer a realistic possibility of success and a sense of personal achievement.

Set your own standards. Don't let others bully you into situations that you know are not right for you or convince you that you should be someone you are not. Don't let the media talk you into believing that the only socially successful people are celebrities and extremely extroverted individuals.

Accentuate the positive. Avoid the tendency of shy individuals to be overly self-critical of their performances in social situations. Showing up—especially showing up early—will allow you to take advantage of the warm-up process and increase the likelihood of a successful performance. You obviously are less likely to experience a sense of social success sitting home alone.

Avoid seeking perfection. You can do much to enhance your sense of social success by being less of a perfectionist and more of a realist. Nobody's perfect, but, out of habit, you may find yourself striving to be perfect anyway.

Your Turn

Describe situations in which you can create opportunities for your own success and the actions you can take to create this success. It is important to realize that the more specific you can be about the situations and the actions you are going to take, the easier it will be to create these opportunities.

1. _____

   _____

   _____

   _____

2. _____

   _____

   _____

   _____

3. _____

   _____

   _____

   _____

4. _____

   _____

   _____

   _____

Voices

"Other people are out there in life having a great time while I sit at home and watch TV, wishing that I was doing other things. I am a very friendly person once people get to know me, but that's just the problem. I'm afraid that I can come off looking like a 'snob' or worse because I don't talk much. I'm not good at first impressions, and I rarely have a second chance to show that I am a nice person."

—a 21-year-old law school student

"Going to several racquetball tournaments was my attempt to overcome my shyness. These tourneys would put me in contact with 30 to 200 players in a weekend. I think I handled it real well. I was able to act outgoing and friendly, even to women players."

—a 41-year-old newspaper editor

'The key to creating opportunities that provide both a sense of success and personal achievement is to control the risks you take.'

Reflections

In the past, have you had trouble controlling the risks you take? Do you think you'll be able to do better in the future?

"The key to creating opportunities that provide both a sense of success and personal achievement is to control the risks you take."

_____

_____

_____

_____

_____

_____

_____

_____

_____

_____

_____

_____

_____

_____

_____

DAY 28 Helping Other Shy Individuals: Becoming a Host to Humanity

What You Need to Know

As you become more successfully shy by controlling your own shyness, it is important for you to help other shy individuals do the same. You can do so by becoming a "host to humanity." The purpose of a host is to help others have a good time. The key to being a good host is to focus less attention on yourself and more attention on others. To do so, you need to perform social graces. Simple social niceties can serve as a mechanism for beginning social interactions with others. There are a number of social graces that you can perform:

You can help people make contact with each other. A good way to start is to approach someone who is standing alone at a social gathering, introduce yourself, and engage in quick talk. Next, when possible, introduce this person to others.

You can try to help others put their best foot forward. Because people feel most confident when discussing topics related to their own interests or expertise, you can help others by finding out what they are interested in or what they know a lot about and then introducing those topics into group conversations.

You can help others keep the conversation going. It's both wise and thoughtful to be sensitive to others who may not be participating in conversations by periodically asking them their opinions and encouraging them to make comments. At the same time, you should keep in mind that you may have to repeat this gesture a few times to account for the warm-up periods of others. By now, it should become clear to you that, in addition to helping others feel more comfortable and confident, focusing your attention on others has the added advantage of making you less self-conscious.

Your Turn

Describe those situations in which you could help others feel more comfortable and confident in social situations and the actions you would take to contribute to their social success.

1. _____

_____

_____

_____

2. _____

_____

_____

_____

3. _____

_____

_____

_____

4. _____

_____

_____

_____

Voices

"Now, greeting customers at my job comes naturally with little anxiety. I smile readily and even enjoy this small exchange. However, I think this is because I'm remaining active (bagging groceries). I'm occupied enough not to be preoccupied with myself."

—a 21-year-old grocery clerk

"My close friends and casual acquaintances would never guess I have any shy feelings at all. I am often the icebreaker for other people who are uncomfortable in social situations. I have inner antennae for other people's shyness. By making them feel more comfortable, I make myself feel more comfortable."

—a 27-year-old high school teacher

‘Simple social graces can serve as a mechanism for beginning social interactions with others.’

Reflections

How can you help others become successfully shy by using simple social graces? Have you followed through on the strategy explained below? If not, do you plan to try it?

"Simple social graces can serve as a mechanism for beginning social interactions with others."

_____

_____

_____

_____

_____

_____

_____

_____

_____

_____

_____

_____

_____

_____

DAY 29 Becoming a Volunteer: Helping Yourself by Helping Others

What You Need to Know

Although it is typically not associated with shyness, volunteerism can help you in your efforts to become successfully shy. Volunteerism, to some people's surprise, offers ready-made solutions for many of the characteristic difficulties experienced by shy individuals.

Serving as a volunteer can help you feel less self-conscious because volunteer work is usually less taxing than regular office or school work. Also, when people help by volunteering, the expectations of their performance are usually more relaxed: You don't have to be an expert—just someone who is willing to help.

In volunteer situations, you are apt to be less self-conscious and self-critical. Because of the reduced stress, you should be able to be yourself and devote more time and attention to the task at hand: helping others.

As you help others by volunteering, you also help yourself to expand your comfort zone. Volunteering enables you to experience new situations without feeling the pressure to perform that you might typically feel in other social situations. Plus, the more you volunteer, the more you will learn about people and things. As a result, you will become more comfortable in a variety of situations—interacting with different kinds of people and discussing different topics. In short, your volunteer experience can help you with many of the basic elements of engaging in successful conversations with others, including initiating, maintaining, and expanding the conversations.

Being a volunteer can help you broaden your social network as well. Inevitably some of the new people you meet through your volunteer activities will become friends with whom you feel comfortable socializing and spending time. Because you have already established a relationship with them through your volunteer efforts, the task of socializing with them will be much easier. It's a win-win situation. You perform volunteer work—helping others and learning responsibility—and in the process, you make new friends.

Your Turn

Describe a number of situations in which you might serve as a volunteer, the actions you would need to take to obtain this volunteer experience, and the benefits you will receive from such volunteerism.

1. _____

_____

_____

_____

2. _____

_____

_____

_____

3. _____

_____

_____

_____

4. _____

_____

_____

_____

Voices

"I have usually belonged to a group or organization in which I would meet and make friends, at least when I was in college. However, when I began my graduate studies at the same school, I suffered from loneliness because I was no longer a part of those groups and I didn't know how to meet people or make new friends."

—a 25-year-old graduate student

"I have become an animal lover and feed and provide shelter to stray cats. I provide them with medical treatment and get them spayed or neutered. I feel very comfortable in this role because I can relate to the people I'm in contact with. I feel very loved and needed. I feel that I am a very kind, warm, and generous person because being shy, I'm sensitive to other people's feelings."

—a 53-year-old secretary

‘Being a volunteer can help you feel less self-conscious.’

Reflections

Make it a point to seek volunteer work. If the following statement is true, and volunteerism does indeed decrease self-consciousness, it certainly sounds like a good idea. Do you think you will give volunteerism a try?

"Being a volunteer can help you feel less self-conscious."

_____

_____

_____

_____

_____

_____

_____

_____

_____

_____

_____

_____

_____

_____

_____

DAY 30 Living the Successfully Shy Life: A Day-to-Day Adventure

What You Need to Know

Helping you to become successfully shy has nothing to do with turning you into an extrovert or changing who you are. Remember: There is nothing wrong with being shy.

The goal of being successfully shy is to ensure that the negative side of your shyness—excessive self-consciousness, overly critical self-evaluation, and self-doubt—no longer limits your choices. To be successfully shy is to live a successful and full life brimming with self-awareness, self-acceptance, and self-confidence. Empowered by these newfound strengths, you will have the insight and courage necessary to change the way you think and the way you go about taking control of your shyness.

One of the keys to becoming successfully shy is to realize that creating a successfully shy life is a day-to-day adventure. To understand how this can be so, think of yourself as a work in progress. Next, instead of thinking of yourself as a shy person, mentally switch labels and think of yourself as a person who is learning how to feel more self-confident so that you can perform more effectively in a greater number of different situations.

Once you've changed labels, it is important that you be patient, that you realize that personal change takes time and effort. To that end, you must be realistic, steadfast, and persistent. You must also remember the past as clearly as possible and look to the future with optimism and self-confidence. Recalling the successes you experienced when you were able to take control of your shyness in past situations will give you the courage to make the necessary changes in present and future situations.

Most important, you should reach beyond your own comfort zone. You should help others overcome their shyness, using strategies you have learned to help individuals you care a great deal about and who are important in your day-to-day life.

You should also share your newfound ideas, knowledge, and experiences with friends, co-workers, loved ones, neighbors, classmates, and relatives. What you will share, among other things, are the following: your new, positive feelings of self-awareness, self-acceptance, and self-confidence. By sharing these robust feelings, you will be showing your friends and loved ones the value of being successfully shy and living a successfully shy life. Incorporating your feelings—and your sharing of those feelings—into your day-to-day living experiences will contribute to your having a full and enriching life. And that's what being successfully shy and living a successfully shy life are all about.

Your Turn

Describe the individuals and situations in your day-to-day life that you would like to have become part of your successfully shy life and the actions you would need to take to do so.

_____

_____

_____

_____

_____

_____

_____

_____

_____

_____

_____

_____

_____

_____

_____

_____

Voices

"As a teenager, I was very painfully shy. I've made great strides and am much less shy now. As my self-confidence grows, I am able to push myself a little more to be more outgoing. It's an ongoing improvement process."

—a 31-year-old pastry chef

"Every once in a while I think that my whole life I've been using shyness as an excuse for inaction. 'I can't do that—I'm shy!' When I feel myself doing that, I am now able to do what I didn't think I could."

—a 23-year-old graduate student

"It was only recently that I began to view my mind as an asset rather than a restriction or handicap. Now that I have honestly evaluated myself and my abilities, I am very confident and only become shy in certain circumstances and around certain people. In fact, because of my confidence, I tend to make others feel shy around me at times. I view that as simply another obstacle to overcome."

—a high school junior

"What I have learned is that I am a strong person with many, many positive attributes. I have nothing to be ashamed of and much to offer others—hence, no need to feel shy. I felt shy as a youngster because of a lack of self-worth. Eventually, I realized my worth and lost my shyness."

—a 55-year-old homemaker

❝Being successfully shy is about living a successful and full life brimming with self-awareness, self-acceptance, and self-confidence.❞

Reflections

How do you feel when you read the comment below? Do you understand the message, and do you feel that you are capable of achieving the goal of being successfully shy?

"Being successfully shy is about living a successful and full life brimming with self-awareness, self-acceptance, and self-confidence."

_____

_____

_____

_____

_____

_____

_____

_____

_____

_____

_____

_____

_____

_____

EPILOGUE   Living a Successfully Shy Life: A Style of Life for Going Beyond Shyness and into the World

What You Need to Know

The Shyness Workbook does not focus on shyness per se. Rather, it contemplates a number of aspects of shyness including its consequences and the lessons it teaches, such as the following: (a) learning the value of volunteerism and stepping out of your comfort zone; (b) becoming successfully shy—learning how to control your shyness rather than allowing your shyness to control you; (c) developing a philosophy of life and a way of living that extend beyond shyness; and (d) empowering you to help not only your shy loved ones, but everyone you can.

The successfully shy life should be no different from any other. All of the processes that you have read about in *The Shyness Workbook*—shyness of the mind and body, slowness to warm up, limited comfort zones, and the approach-avoidance conflict—are part of human nature. Although they are common to everyone, they seem more salient for shy people.

I am hopeful that your involvement with *The Shyness Workbook* will make it possible for you to greet the world on your own terms and help those around you—the shy and the bold alike. Remember the value of social skills, social graces, and small talk. These attributes not only help you relate to others more graciously, they also help society function more smoothly. They make people feel more comfortable, and when people are not anxious or distressed, they find it much easier to behave naturally rather than reactively. Living a successfully shy life is good for you and for those around you. It makes the world a better place.

As you complete *The Shyness Workbook,* keep in mind that this is not the end of your involvement with it, but merely the beginning of *your successfully shy life.* Good luck, take care, and keep in touch.

Best regards,
Bernardo J. Carducci, Ph.D.

The Shyness Enrichment Institute
P.O. Box 8064
New Albany, IN 47151–8064
shydoc@carducci.com
www.ius.edu/shyness

Your Turn

Describe the kinds of changes you will make in your life and the impact these changes will have on others as you begin to live a successfully shy life.

_____

_____

_____

_____

_____

_____

_____

_____

_____

_____

_____

_____

_____

_____

_____

_____

_____

Voices

"I was very shy as a kid—shy and extremely neurotic. Every situation scared me if it required my interacting with others. Luckily, I had my twin sister with me a lot of the time and we fed off each other in order to survive through any interaction. After high school and into college, I became much less shy. I consciously made each interaction an 'exercise' in overcoming my shyness. Just talking to people I didn't know, hanging out with people without my sister, getting a part-time job, volunteering at different places. I had always been afraid to sing in front of people I wasn't related to, but now I sing all the time everywhere. That was a big deal to me."

—a successfully shy college student

"I find the best way to overcome shyness is to take the first step and face the fear that brings on the shyness. It isn't easy; I still get my heart racing and beating so loud. I almost feel the person next to me can hear it pounding. I volunteer for presentations and get involved in projects I enjoy. Interestingly, I found that I was not shy during my volunteer work for the World Cup soccer games. I believe the reason is that I did something from my heart. So perhaps the way to overcome shyness is to do something one really loves, and little by little the shyness will be diminished by the act itself."

—a successfully shy volunteer

'As you complete *The Shyness Workbook,* keep in mind that this is only the beginning of your involvement with learning to live *your successfully shy life.*'

Reflections

Do you agree with the following statement, and do you believe strongly that you can enjoy a successfully shy life?

As you complete *The Shyness Workbook*, keep in mind that this is not the end of your involvement with it, but merely the beginning of *your successfully shy life.*

_____

_____

_____

_____

_____

_____

_____

_____

_____

_____

_____

_____

_____

_____

SELECTED BIBLIOGRAPHY

If you would like more information about shyness and the topics discussed in *The Shyness Workbook,* I recommend that you go to the Indiana University Southeast Shyness Research Institute Web site at www.isu.edu/shyness or read any of the following:

Carducci, B. J. (1999). *The Pocket Guide to making successful small talk: How to talk to anyone anytime anywhere about anything.* New Albany, IN: Pocket Guide Publishing.

Carducci, B. J. (2000a). *Shyness: A bold new approach.* New York: HarperPerennial.

Carducci, B. J. (2000b). Shyness: The new solution. *Psychology Today, 33,* 38–40, 42–45, & 78.

Carducci, B. J. (2000c). What shy individuals do to cope with their shyness: A content analysis. In W. R. Crozier (Ed.), *Shyness: development, consolidation, and change* (pp. 171–185). New York: Routledge.

Carducci, B. J. (2001). Are we born shy? *The Psychology Place* [On line, Archive: Op Ed Forum, February 2001]. Available: http://psychplace.com/archives/editorials.

Carducci, B. J. (2003). *The shyness breakthrough: A no-stress plan to help your shy child warm up, open up, and join the fun.* Emmaus, PA: Rodale.

Carducci, B. J., & Zimbardo, P. G. (1995, November/ December). Are you shy? *Psychology Today, 28,* 34–41, 64, 66, 68, 70, 78, 82.

Zimbardo, P. G. (1990). *Shyness: What it is, what to do about it* (Reissued ed.). Reading, MA: Addison-Wesley.

Zimbardo, P. G., & Radl, S. L. (1999). *The shy child: A parent's guide to preventing and overcoming shyness in infancy to adulthood* (2nd ed.). Cambridge, MA: Malor Books.

About the Author

Bernardo J. Carducci (Ph.D., Kansas State University, 1981) is a full professor of psychology and director of the Shyness Research Institute at Indiana University Southeast; Fellow of the American Psychological Association and a member of *Who's Who in Frontier Science and Technology;* and a consultant with Social Performance Enhancement Services.

In addition to *The Shyness Workbook,* he has authored the following books: *The Pocket Guide to Making Successful Small Talk: How to Talk to Anyone Anytime Anywhere About Anything* (1999, Pocket Guide Publishing); *Shyness: A Bold New Approach* (2000a, HarperPerennial); *The Shyness Breakthrough: A No-Stress Plan to Help Your Shy Child Warm Up, Open Up, and Join the Fun* (2003, Rodale); and the college textbook *The Psychology of Personality: Viewpoints, Research, and Applications* (1998, BrooksCole).

Dr. Carducci has appeared numerous times on ABC-TV's *Good Morning America* and other national and international broadcast media, such as the BBC. His writings and advice have been featured in a number of diverse magazines and newspapers, including, among others, *Psychology Today, U.S. News & World Report, USA Weekend, Vogue, Allure, YM, TWA Ambassador, Glamour, JET, Parenting, WebMD, Walking, Good Housekeeping, JANE, Essence, Child, Reader's Digest, Parents, Redbook, Real Simple, First for Women, The Futurist, Entrepreneur, Fitness, The Chicago Tribune, The Wall Street Journal, The London Times, The Los Angeles Times,* and *The New York Times.*